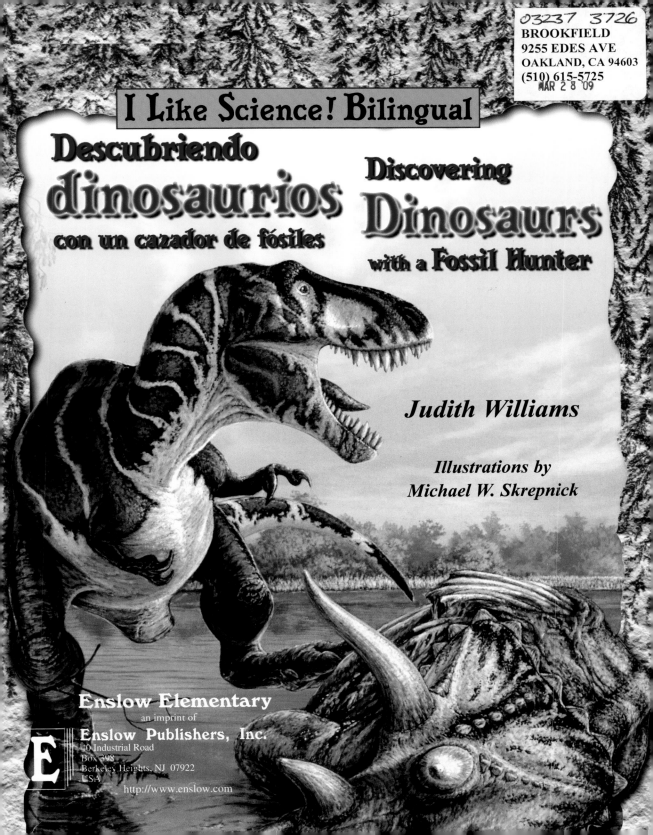

I Like Science! Bilingual

Descubriendo dinosaurios con un cazador de fósiles

Discovering Dinosaurs with a Fossil Hunter

Judith Williams

Illustrations by
Michael W. Skrepnick

Enslow Elementary
an imprint of
Enslow Publishers, Inc.
40 Industrial Road
Box 398
Berkeley Heights, NJ 07922
USA
http://www.enslow.com

Contents

Contenido

Words to know/Palabras a conocer

fossil (FOSS ul)—What is left from a plant or animal that lived long ago.
fósil—Lo que queda de una planta o animal que vivió hace mucho tiempo.

pack (PAK)—A group of animals that lives and hunts together, like wolves
manada—Un grupo de animales que viven y cazan juntos, como los lobos.

paleontologist (pail ee on TOL oh gist)—A scientist who studies fossils and life from long ago.
paleontólogo—Científico que estudia fósiles y la vida de hace mucho tiempo atrás.

plaster (PLAS tur)—A powder mixed with water that gets hard when it dries.
yeso—Polvo que se mezcla con agua y se endurece al secar.

skeleton (SKEL a ton)—All the bones that make up an animal's body.
esqueleto—Todos los huesos que forman el cuerpo de un animal.

tyrannosaur (tie RAN oh sor)—A kind of meat-eating dinosaur, such as *T. rex*.
tiranosaurio—Tipo de dinosaurio carnívoro, como el *T. rex*.

How do we find out facts about dinosaurs?

Scientists start by asking questions.

How is one dinosaur different from another? What things are the same? That is how scientists learn!

¿Cómo obtenemos información sobre los dinosaurios?

Los científicos empiezan haciendo preguntas.

¿En qué se diferencia un dinosaurio de otro? ¿En qué se parecen? ¡Así aprenden los científicos!

duck-billed dinosaurs

dinosaurios con pico de pato

Meet paleontologist Phil Currie.

He is a dinosaur scientist. He has liked dinosaurs since he was young. Now, learning about them is his job.

What does he do?

Éste es el paleontólog Phil Currie.

Es científico de dinosaurios. Desde que era niño le gustan los dinosaurios. Ahora, aprender acerca de ellos es su trabajo.

¿Qué hace?

4

He finds
fossils and
measures
bones.
He sorts
the facts.
He wants
to know
how
dinosaurs
lived.

dinosaur
footprint

huella de
dinosaurio

Encuentra fósiles y
mide huesos. Analiza los
datos. Quiere saber
cómo vivieron los
dinosaurios.

5

How are fossils found?

Paleontologists look for bones lying on the ground. Often, only part of the fossil shows.

Gobi Desert in Asia / Desierto Gobi en Asia

¿Cómo se encuentran los fósiles?

Los paleontólogos buscan huesos que están en el suelo. Muchas veces sólo encuentran una parte del fósil.

6

If they dig, they might get lucky
and find the rest of the
skeleton.

Si excavan, pueden tener suerte
y encontrar el resto del
esqueleto.

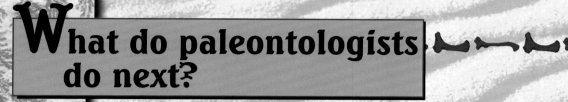

What do paleontologists do next?

They cover the fossils in wet plaster. When the plaster dries, it turns hard.

Then the fossil is safe to be moved.

¿Qué hacen enseguida los paleontólogos?

Cubren los fósiles con yeso húmedo. Cuando el yeso se seca, se pone duro.

Entonces es seguro mover el fósil.

dinosaur bone inside

huesos de dinosaurio dentro

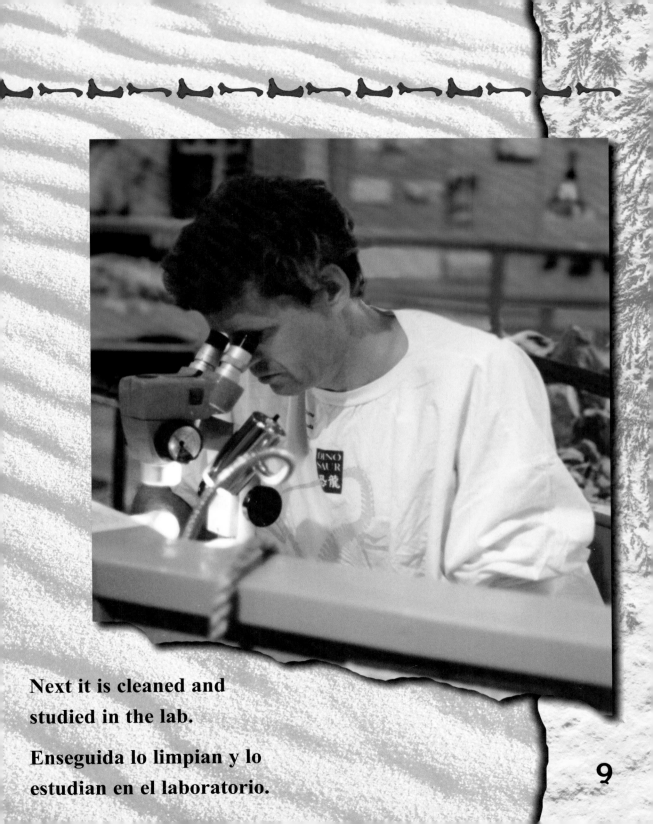

Next it is cleaned and
studied in the lab.

Enseguida lo limpian y lo
estudian en el laboratorio.

What do fossils show us?

Fossils tell stories about dinosaur lives. Each bone and tooth shows many things.

¿Qué nos muestran los fósiles?

Los fósiles cuentan historias sobre la vida de los dinosaurios. Cada hueso y cada diente muestra muchas cosas.

Diplodocus (dih PLAHD oh kus) family

familia Diplodocus

To paleontologists, bones answer questions. If you were a paleontologist, what questions would *you* ask?

Para los paleontólogos, los huesos responden preguntas. Si tú fueras paleontólogo, ¿qué preguntas harías?

11

Did dinosaurs come from eggs?

Yes, just like birds, dinosaurs laid eggs.

¿Los dinosaurios eran ovíparos?

Sí, igual que los pájaros, los dinosaurios ponían huevos.

Titanosaurus (tie TAN oh sor us)
Titanosaurio

12

In one place, scientists found hundreds of fossil nests. Each nest had many eggs. That is a lot of baby dinosaurs!

dinosaur eggs in nest

huevos de dinosaurio en un nido

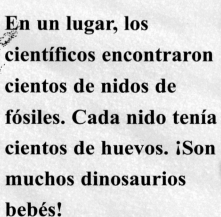

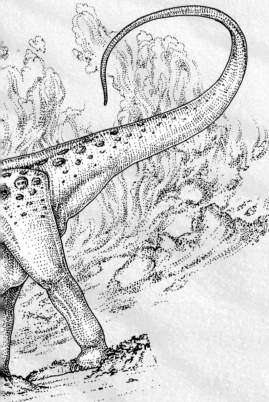

En un lugar, los científicos encontraron cientos de nidos de fósiles. Cada nido tenía cientos de huevos. ¡Son muchos dinosaurios bebés!

Did all baby dinosaurs stay in the nest?

Maybe they did not. Meat-eating dinosaurs may have left the nest after they hatched. They could run. They could hunt. They were busy right away!

Tyrannosaurus babies may have had feathers.

Los bebés de tiranosaurio pueden haber tenido plumas.

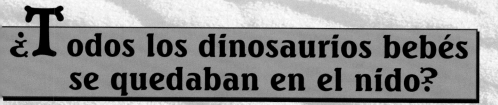

¿Todos los dinosaurios bebés se quedaban en el nido?

Quizá no. Los dinosaurios carnívoros pueden haber dejado el nido después de salir del huevo. Podían correr. Podían cazar. ¡De inmediato tenían cosas que hacer!

Did all dinosaurs eat meat?

No, most dinosaurs ate only plants. Scientists look at plant fossils. The fossils show what these dinosaurs ate.

¿Todos los dinosaurios eran carnívoros?

Iguanodon
(ih GWAHN oh don)

Iguanodonte

No, la mayoría de los dinosaurios sólo comían plantas. Los científicos analizan los fósiles de plantas. Los fósiles muestran qué comían estos dinosaurios.

Some dinosaurs ate meat—usually other dinosaurs. But they would eat any animal they could catch.

Algunos dinosaurios comían carne, usualmente se alimentaban de otros dinosaurios. Pero comían cualquier animal que pudieran atrapar.

Gorgosaurus (GOR goh SOR us)
Gorgosaurio

Centrosaurus (SEN troh SOR us)
Centrosaurio

Did meat-eating dinosaurs live in groups?

Paleontologist Phil found many tyrannosaur fossils in one place. Some were young. Some were adults.

¿Los dinosaurios carnívoros vivían en grupos?

El paleontólogo Phil encontró muchos fósiles de tiranosaurios en un mismo lugar. Algunos eran jóvenes. Algunos eran adultos.

Hypacrosaurus (hie PAK roh SOR us)
Hypacrosaurio

18

He thinks these dinosaurs lived in groups, called packs. Maybe young dinosaurs helped the adults hunt.

Él piensa que estos dinosaurios vivían en grupos, llamados manadas. Quizá los dinosaurios jóvenes ayudaban a los adultos a cazar.

Albertosaurus (al BURT oh SOR us) pack

Manada de albertosaurios

Paleontologists like Phil Currie are busy thinking of many more questions about dinosaurs. They are looking for answers, too. Good-bye, paleontologist Phil, and good luck!

Los paleontólogos como Phil Currie están ocupados pensando en muchas más preguntas acerca de los dinosaurios. También buscan respuestas. Adiós, paleontólogo Phil, y ¡buena suerte!

How are plant fossils formed?

cks press down on plants, just as they did on dinosaur
mes. You can see how this works.

Take two sheets of plain
ite paper. Put a leaf
ween the sheets of
per.

2. With a colored pencil, color the
top sheet over the leaf.

1.

The shape looks like a
nt fossil.

Well done!

¿Cómo se forman los fósiles de planta?

Las rocas presionan las plantas, igual que lo hicieron con los huesos de los dinosaurios. Puedes ver cómo funciona.

1. Toma dos hojas de papel blanco sencillo. Coloca una hoja de árbol entre las hojas de papel.

2. Con un lápiz de color colorea la hoja de papel de arriba sobre la hoja del árbol.

3. La forma se parece a un fósil de planta.

2.

3.

¡Bien hecho!

Learn More / Más para aprender

Books / Libros

In English / En inglés

Gibbons, Gail. *Dinosaur Discoveries*. New York: Holiday House, 2005.

MacLeod, Elizabeth. *What Did Dinosaurs Eat? And Other Things You Want to Know About Dinosaurs*. Toronto, Canada: Kids Can Press, 2001.

Taylor, Barbara. *Oxford First Book of Dinosaurs*. Oxford, New York: Oxford University Press, 2001.

In Spanish / En español

Lessem, "Dino" Don. *Herbívoros gigantes*. Minneapolis, Minn.: Ediciones Lerner, 2006.

Mattern, Joanne. *Dinosaurios, espinas óseas y cuellos*. Milwaukee, Wisc.: Weekly Reader Early Learning Library, 2005.

Internet Addresses / Direcciones de Internet

In English / En inglés

National Geographic Kids
<http://www.nationalgeographic.com/ngkids/0005/dino/>

KidsDinos.com
<http://www.kidsdinos.com/>

In English and Spanish / En inglés y español
<http://www.childrensmuseum.org/dinosphere/kids/kids_activities.html>

Index

Índice

❂ *For Michael* ❂

Series Literacy Consultant:
Allan A. De Fina, Ph.D.
Past President of the New Jersey Reading Association
Professor, Department of Literacy Education
New Jersey City University

Science Consultant:
Philip J. Currie, Ph.D., Curator of Dinosaur Research
Royal Tyrrell Museum, Alberta, Canada
Dr. Currie says, "I wish there had been a book like this when I was young!"

Note to Teachers and Parents: The *I Like Science!* series supports the National Science Education Standards for K-4 science, including content standards "Science as a human endeavor" and "Science as inquiry." The Words to Know section introduces subject-specific vocabulary, including pronunciation and definitions. Early readers may require help with these new words.

Enslow Elementary, an imprint of Enslow Publishers, Inc.
Enslow Elementary® is a registered trademark of Enslow Publishers, Inc.

Bilingual edition copyright 2008 by Enslow Publishers, Inc. Originally published in English under the title *Discovering Dinosaurs with a Fossil Hunter* © 2004 by Enslow Publishers, Inc. Bilingual edition translated by Nora Díaz, edited by María Cristina Mella, of Strictly Spanish, LLC.

Copyright © 2008 by Enslow Publishers, Inc.

Library of Congress Cataloging-in-Publication Data

Williams, Judith (Judith A.)

[Discovering dinosaurs with a fossil hunter. Spanish & English]

Descubriendo dinosaurios con un cazador de fósiles = Discovering dinosaurs with a fossil hunter / Judith Williams; illustrations by Michael W. Skrepnick.—Bilingual ed.
    p. cm.— (I like science! Bilingual)
    Summary: "Discusses dinosaurs and what can be learned from their fossils"—Provided by publisher.
    Includes bibliographical references and index.
    ISBN-13: 978-0-7660-2978-1
    ISBN-10:   0-7660-2978-6

1. Paleontology—Juvenile literature. 2. Fossils—Juvenile literature. I. Skrepnick, Michael William, ill. II. Title.

QE714.5.W5518 2008
567.9—dc22   2007011586

Printed in the United States of America
10 9 8 7 6 5 4 3 2 1

To Our Readers: We have done our best to make sure all Internet Addresses in this book were active and appropriate when we went to press. However, the author and the publisher have no control over and assume no liability for the material available on those Internet sites or on other Web sites they may link to. Any comments or suggestions can be sent by e-mail to comments@enslow.com or to the address on the back cover.

Illustration Credits: © Michael W. Skrepnick

All Photos © Michael W. Skrepnick 1990–2003, except Neg. no. 18552, Courtesy the Library, American Museum of Natural History, p. 2; Judith Williams, p. 4.

Cover Illustration: Michael W. Skrepnick
Tyrannosaurus and *Triceratops*